EASY CRACKER COOKBOOK

50 DELICIOUS CRACKER RECIPES; SIMPLE TECHNIQUES FOR COOKING WITH CRACKERS

By
BookSumo Press

Published by
BookSumo Press, a DBA of Saxonberg Associates
http://www.booksumo.com/

ABOUT THE AUTHOR.

BookSumo Press is a publisher of unique, easy, and healthy cookbooks.

Our cookbooks span all topics and all subjects. If you want a deep dive into the possibilities of cooking with any type of ingredient. Then BookSumo Press is your go to place for robust yet simple and delicious cookbooks and recipes. Whether you are looking for great tasting pressure cooker recipes or authentic ethic and cultural food. BookSumo Press has a delicious and easy cookbook for you.

With simple ingredients, and even simpler step-by-step instructions BookSumo cookbooks get everyone in the kitchen chefing delicious meals.

BookSumo is an independent publisher of books operating in the beautiful Garden State (NJ) and our team of chefs and kitchen experts are here to teach, eat, and be merry!

INTRODUCTION

Welcome to *The Effortless Chef Series*! Thank you for taking the time to purchase this cookbook.

Come take a journey into the delights of easy cooking. The point of this cookbook and all BookSumo Press cookbooks is to exemplify the effortless nature of cooking simply.

In this book we focus on Crackers. You will find that even though the recipes are simple, the taste of the dishes are quite amazing.

So will you take an adventure in simple cooking? If the answer is yes please consult the table of contents to find the dishes you are most interested in.

Once you are ready, jump right in and start cooking.

— BookSumo Press

TABLE OF CONTENTS

ANY ISSUES? CONTACT US

If you find that something important to you is missing from this book please contact us at info@booksumo.com.

We will take your concerns into consideration when the 2nd edition of this book is published. And we will keep you updated!

— BookSumo Press

LEGAL NOTES

COMMON ABBREVIATIONS

cup(s)	C.
tablespoon	tbsp
teaspoon	tsp
ounce	oz.
pound	lb

*All units used are standard American measurements

Chapter 1: Easy Cracker Recipes

Semi-Sweet Crackers

Ingredients

- 1/4 (16 oz.) package saltine crackers
- 1/2 lb. butter
- 3/4 C. white sugar
- 2 C. semisweet chocolate chips
- 3/4 C. chopped walnuts

Directions

- Set your oven to 425 degrees F before doing anything else.
- In a pan, melt the butter on medium heat.
- Stir in the sugar and bring to a gentle boil.
- Boil for about 3 minutes, stirring continuously.
- In a cookie sheet, arrange the crackers in a single layer and drizzle with the sugar mixture evenly.
- Cook in the oven for about 5 minutes.
- Remove from oven and immediately, spread the chocolate chips over crackers to melt.
- Spread the walnuts on top and gently press into the melted chocolate.

- Keep aside till the chocolate becomes hard.
- Break into desired sized pieces and refrigerate till serving.

Amount per serving 10

Timing Information:

Preparation	5 m
Cooking	10 m
Total Time	30 m

Nutritional Information:

Calories	598 kcal
Fat	39 g
Carbohydrates	58.2g
Protein	6 g
Cholesterol	49 mg
Sodium	251 mg

* Percent Daily Values are based on a 2,000 calorie diet.

GARDEN PARTY CRACKERS

Ingredients

- 1 (12 oz.) package oyster crackers
- 1 (1 oz.) package French dressing mix
- 1/2 tsp dried tarragon
- 1/4 tsp garlic powder
- 3/4 C. vegetable oil

Directions

- Set your oven to 200 degrees F before doing anything else.
- In a bowl, add the oil and seasonings and beat well.
- Add the crackers and toss to coat well.
- In a large baking sheet, spread the crackers evenly.
- Cook in the oven for about 20 minutes, stirring once after 10 minutes.

Amount per serving 12

Timing Information:

Preparation	10 m
Cooking	20 m
Total Time	30 m

Nutritional Information:

Calories	256 kcal
Fat	18.8 g
Carbohydrates	19.4g
Protein	2.3 g
Cholesterol	0 mg
Sodium	699 mg

* Percent Daily Values are based on a 2,000 calorie diet.

Buttery Retreat Snack

Ingredients

- 2 C. all-purpose flour
- 1 pinch salt
- 1 1/2 tsp red pepper flakes
- 1 lb. Monterey cheese, grated and room temperature
- 1 C. unsalted butter, melted
- 2 C. crispy rice cereal (such as Rice Krispies(R))

Directions

- Set your oven to 300 degrees F before doing anything else.
- In a large bowl, mix together the flour, salt and red pepper flakes.
- Add the Monterey cheese and toss to coat well.
- Add the melted butter and stir till moist and crumbly.
- Add the rice cereal and with your hands, knead till a dough is formed.
- Make small 1/2-inch balls from the dough.
- Place the balls onto a baking sheet in a single layer and with a fork, flatten each ball.
- Cook in the oven for about 30 minutes.

Amount per serving 150

Timing Information:

Preparation	15 m
Cooking	30 m
Total Time	45 m

Nutritional Information:

Calories	31 kcal
Fat	2.3 g
Carbohydrates	1.7g
Protein	1 g
Cholesterol	6 mg
Sodium	24 mg

* Percent Daily Values are based on a 2,000 calorie diet.

Simple Saltines with Chili Powder

Ingredients

- 1 1/2 C. canola oil
- 2 tbsp crushed red pepper flakes
- 1 (1 oz.) packet ranch dressing mix
- 1 tbsp chili powder
- 1 (16 oz.) package Whole Wheat Saltine Crackers

Directions

- In a bowl, add the canola oil, crushed red pepper flakes, ranch dressing mix and chili powder and beat till well combined.
- Divide the crackers and oil mixture in 2 (1-gallon) sealable bags evenly.
- Seal the bag and flip, then keep aside for about 5 minutes.
- Keep aside for about 1 hour, flipping after every 5 minutes.
- Now, transfer the crackers onto large platters and keep aside for overnight before serving.

Amount per serving 30

Timing Information:

Preparation	10 m
Total Time	9 h 10 m

Nutritional Information:

Calories	169 kcal
Fat	13.3 g
Carbohydrates	11.2g
Protein	1.7 g
Cholesterol	0 mg
Sodium	223 mg

* Percent Daily Values are based on a 2,000 calorie diet.

OYSTER CRACKER CLASSIC

Ingredients

- 1 (1 oz.) package ranch dressing mix
- 1 tsp garlic powder
- 1/2 tsp dried dill weed
- 1/2 C. vegetable oil
- 1 (12 oz.) package oyster crackers

Directions

- In a bowl, mix together the ranch dressing mix, garlic powder, dill and vegetable oil.
- Add the crackers and gently, mix to coat.
- Keep aside for about 1 hour, stirring after every 10 minutes.
- Transfer the crackers in an airtight jar to store.

Amount per serving 12

Timing Information:

Preparation	1 h 5 m
Cooking	1 h 5 m
Total Time	1 h 5 m

Nutritional Information:

Calories	217 kcal
Fat	14.2 g
Carbohydrates	19.6g
Protein	2.3 g
Cholesterol	0 mg
Sodium	699 mg

* Percent Daily Values are based on a 2,000 calorie diet.

KETOGENIC SPINACH AND COCONUT CRACKERS

Ingredients

- 1 tbsp coconut oil
- 4 tsp chopped onion
- 2 cloves garlic, minced
- 3 1/2 tbsp chopped fresh mushrooms
- 1 tbsp frozen chopped spinach, thawed and drained
- 1/3 C. almond flour
- 1/3 C. coconut flour
- 2 tbsp flax seed meal
- 1/2 tsp salt
- 1 pinch ground black pepper
- 2 eggs
- 2 tbsp water
- 1 tbsp olive oil

Directions

- In a skillet, melt the coconut oil on medium heat and sauté the onion and garlic for about 5 minutes.
- Add the mushrooms and sauté for about 5 minutes.

- Stir in the spinach and cook for about 2-3 minutes.
- Remove from the heat and keep aside to cool slightly.
- In a bowl, mix together the flours, flax seed meal, salt and pepper.
- Transfer vegetable mixture to a work cutting board and chop it finely.
- Add the chopped vegetable mixture into the flour mixture and stir to combine.
- Add the eggs, water and olive oil and mix till a dough is formed.
- Set your oven to 425 degrees F before doing anything else and line a baking dish with the parchment paper.
- Place the dough onto the prepared baking sheet.
- Shape the dough into a flat rectangle and press to flatten evenly.
- Arrange a second parchment paper over the dough.
- Roll the dough into 1/16-inch thickness.
- Remove top parchment paper and cut the extra edges of dough to make an even rectangle.
- Place the excess dough to 1 end of the rectangle and re-roll into even thickness.
- With a pizza cutter, cut the dough into 1-inch squares.
- Cook in the oven for about 18-20 minutes.
- Remove from the oven and keep aside to cool completely.
- Break the baked dough into squares.

Amount per serving 16

Timing Information:

Preparation	30 m
Cooking	30 m
Total Time	1 h 30 m

Nutritional Information:

Calories	50 kcal
Fat	3.2 g
Carbohydrates	4g
Protein	1.7 g
Cholesterol	23 mg
Sodium	82 mg

* Percent Daily Values are based on a 2,000 calorie diet.

TROPICAL SPREAD

Ingredients

- 1 (6 oz.) can crabmeat
- 1 (8 oz.) package cream cheese, softened
- 1 (8 oz.) can crushed pineapple
- 4 dashes Worcestershire sauce
- 2 tbsp ketchup
- 1 pinch garlic powder

Directions

- In a bowl, mix together the crab meat and cream cheese.
- Add the pineapple, Worcestershire sauce, ketchup and garlic powder and mix well.
- Refrigerate for overnight.
- This crab mixture is best to be served over the croakers of your choice.

Amount per serving 5

Timing Information:

Preparation	8 h 5 m
Total Time	8 h 5 m

Nutritional Information:

Calories	223 kcal
Fat	16.1 g
Carbohydrates	9.9g
Protein	10.6 g
Cholesterol	79 mg
Sodium	315 mg

* Percent Daily Values are based on a 2,000 calorie diet.

SIMPLE PICNIC CRACKERS

Ingredients

- 1/2 (16 oz.) package graham crackers
- 2 C. chopped pecans
- 1/2 C. white sugar
- 1/2 C. butter
- 1/2 C. margarine

Directions

- Set your oven to 350 degrees F before doing anything else.
- Arrange the graham crackers onto a baking sheet evenly and sprinkle with the pecans.
- In a small pan, mix together the sugar, butter and margarine on medium heat and bring to a boil.
- Boil for about 3 minutes.
- Remove from the heat and place the mixture over pecans, coating well.
- Cook in the oven for about 12 minutes.
- Remove from the oven and keep aside to cool completely before serving.

Amount per serving 25

Timing Information:

Preparation	10 m
Cooking	12 m
Total Time	22 m

Nutritional Information:

Calories	178 kcal
Fat	14.5 g
Carbohydrates	12.1g
Protein	1.5 g
Cholesterol	10 mg
Sodium	122 mg

* Percent Daily Values are based on a 2,000 calorie diet.

Atlanta Style Salad

Ingredients

- 12 oz. saltine crackers
- 3 tomatoes - peeled, seeded and diced
- 1 onion, finely diced
- 1 green bell pepper, diced
- 1 (8 oz.) package sharp Cheddar cheese, shredded
- 1/4 C. mayonnaise, or as needed

Directions

- In a bowl, break the saltines into pieces.
- Add the tomatoes, onion, green bell pepper, cheddar cheese, mayonnaise, salt and pepper and mix well.
- Refrigerate to chill before serving.

Amount per serving 6

Timing Information:

Preparation	10 m
Total Time	10 m

Nutritional Information:

Calories	481 kcal
Fat	26.2 g
Carbohydrates	46g
Protein	15.6 g
Cholesterol	43 mg
Sodium	889 mg

* Percent Daily Values are based on a 2,000 calorie diet.

ELEMENTARY SCHOOL LUNCH CRACKERS

Ingredients

- 2 C. all-purpose flour
- 1 tsp salt
- 1/4 tsp ground white pepper
- 1/4 tsp dry mustard
- 3/4 C. butter, chilled
- 1/2 C. shredded Cheddar cheese
- 6 tbsp cold water, or as needed

Directions

- In a bowl, mix together the flour, salt, white pepper and mustard.
- With a fork, cut in the butter till a coarse crumbs like mixture forms.
- Stir in the Cheddar cheese.
- Slowly, add the water, 1 tbsp at a time and mix till a dough forms.
- Shape the dough into a ball.
- Wrap the ball and refrigerate for at least 30 minutes.

- Set your oven to 350 degrees F and line baking sheets with the parchment papers.
- Place the dough onto a lightly floured surface and roll into 1/8 inch thickness.
- Shape the rolled dough into a 16x12-inch rectangle and then cut into 1x3-inch strips.
- Arrange the strips onto the prepared baking sheets about- 1 inch apart.
- Cook in the oven for about 10-12 minutes.
- Remove from the oven and keep aside to cool completely before storing.

Amount per serving 48

Timing Information:

Preparation	15 m
Cooking	10 m
Total Time	55 m

Nutritional Information:

Calories	50 kcal
Fat	3.4 g
Carbohydrates	4g
Protein	0.9 g
Cholesterol	9 mg
Sodium	78 mg

* Percent Daily Values are based on a 2,000 calorie diet.

ARTISANAL HANDMADE CRACKERS

Ingredients

- 1/2 C. shortening
- 3/4 C. packed brown sugar
- 1 tsp vanilla extract
- 2 C. whole wheat flour
- 1 C. all-purpose flour
- 1 tsp baking powder
- 1/2 tsp baking soda
- 1/4 tsp salt
- 1/4 C. milk

Directions

- In a bowl, add the shortening and brown sugar and beat till creamy.
- Add the vanilla and stir to combine.
- In another bowl, mix together the flours, baking powder, baking soda and salt.
- Add the flour mixture into the shortening mixture alternately with the milk and mix till well combined.
- Refrigerate, covered to chill till firm.

- Set your oven to 350 degrees F and grease the cookie sheets.
- Place the dough onto a lightly floured surface.
- Roll the dough into 1/8-inch thickness and then cut into rectangles.
- Arrange the rectangles onto the prepared cookie sheets about 1/2-inch apart.
- Cook in the oven for about 10-12 minutes.
- Remove from the oven and keep aside to cool completely before serving.

Amount per serving 24

Timing Information:

Preparation	30m
Total Time	50m

Nutritional Information:

Calories	119 kcal
Fat	4.6 g
Carbohydrates	18.2g
Protein	2 g
Cholesterol	< 1 mg
Sodium	74 mg

* Percent Daily Values are based on a 2,000 calorie diet.

TODDLER'S CHOICE CRACKERS

Ingredients

- 1/2 C. rolled oats
- 3/4 C. all-purpose flour
- 1/4 tsp baking soda
- 1/4 tsp salt
- 1/4 C. butter
- 2 tsp honey
- 1/4 C. buttermilk

Directions

- Set your oven to 400 degrees F before doing anything else.
- In a food processor, grind the oats finely.
- In a bowl, mix together the blended oats, flour, baking soda and salt.
- With a pastry blender, cut in the butter till the butter lumps are smaller than peas.
- Add the buttermilk and honey and stir till a stiff dough forms.
- Place the dough onto a lightly floured surface.

- Roll the dough into 1/8-inch thickness and then with cookie cutters, cut into desired shapes.
- Arrange the cookies onto the prepared cookie sheets about 1-inch apart.
- Cook in the oven for about 5-7 minutes.
  - Remove from the oven and keep aside to cool completely before serving.

Amount per serving 24

Timing Information:

Preparation	30 m
Cooking	10 m
Total Time	42 m

Nutritional Information:

Calories	40 kcal
Fat	2.1 g
Carbohydrates	4.8g
Protein	0.7 g
Cholesterol	5 mg
Sodium	54 mg

* Percent Daily Values are based on a 2,000 calorie diet.

A CATERER'S BEST FRIEND

Ingredients

- 1 lb. bittersweet chocolate
- 80 buttery round crackers
- 1/2 tsp peppermint extract

Directions

- With a double boiler method, melt the chocolate coatings over boiling water for about 15-20 minutes, stirring occasionally.
- Add a couple drops of peppermint flavor into the chocolate and stir to combine.
- Coat the crackers into the melted chocolate evenly.
- Arrange the coated crackers onto a cold cookie sheet in a single layer and refrigerate till set.
- Transfer the crackers in candy C.
- Place these crackers in an airtight container and keep at room temperature to preserve.

Amount per serving 40

Timing Information:

Preparation	
Cooking	
Total Time	

Nutritional Information:

Calories	100 kcal
Fat	5.8 g
Carbohydrates	10.6g
Protein	1.2 g
Cholesterol	< 1 mg
Sodium	65 mg

* Percent Daily Values are based on a 2,000 calorie diet.

ENGLISH HANDMADE OAT CRACKERS

Ingredients

- 1 1/2 C. rolled oats
- 1 C. whole wheat flour
- 1/2 tsp salt
- 1 tbsp white sugar
- 1 tsp ground cinnamon (optional)
- 1/2 C. water
- 5 tbsp olive oil

Directions

- Set your oven to 350 degrees F before doing anything else and grease a baking sheet.
- In a food processor, add the rolled oats and pulse till a coarse flour forms.
- Transfer the oat flour into a bowl with the whole wheat flour, salt, sugar, and cinnamon and mix.
- Add the water and olive oil and till a soft dough forms.
- Place the dough onto a lightly floured surface.
- Roll the dough into 1/8-inch thickness and cut into desired shapes.

- Arrange the dough pieces onto prepared baking sheet in a single layer.
- Cook in the oven for about 10-15 minutes.
- Remove from the oven and keep aside to cool completely before serving.

Amount per serving 36

Timing Information:

Preparation	10 m
Cooking	10 m
Total Time	40 m

Nutritional Information:

Calories	42 kcal
Fat	2.2 g
Carbohydrates	5.1g
Protein	0.9 g
Cholesterol	0 mg
Sodium	33 mg

* Percent Daily Values are based on a 2,000 calorie diet.

How to Make Crackers

Ingredients

- 1 3/4 C. whole wheat flour
- 1 1/2 C. all-purpose flour
- 3/4 tsp salt
- 1/3 C. vegetable oil
- 1 C. water
- salt for sprinkling

Directions

- Set your oven to 350 degrees F before doing anything else.
- In a bowl, mix together the flours and 3/4 tsp of the salt.
- Add the vegetable oil and water and mix till just combined.
- Place the dough onto a lightly floured surface.
- Roll the dough into 1/8 inch thickness.
- Arrange the rolled dough onto an ungreased baking sheet and with a knife, mark the squares.
- With a fork, prick each cracker a few times and sprinkle with the salt.
- Cook in the oven for about 15-20 minutes.

- Remove from the oven and keep aside to cool completely before serving.
- Carefully, remove from the baking sheet and separate into individual crackers.

Amount per serving 32

Timing Information:

Preparation	10 m
Cooking	20 m
Total Time	30 m

Nutritional Information:

Calories	64 kcal
Fat	2.5 g
Carbohydrates	9.2g
Protein	1.5 g
Cholesterol	0 mg
Sodium	55 mg

* Percent Daily Values are based on a 2,000 calorie diet.

LEMON PEPPER CRACKERS

Ingredients

- 1 (1 oz.) package Ranch-style dressing mix
- 1/2 tsp dried dill weed
- 1/4 C. vegetable oil
- 1/4 tsp lemon pepper (optional)
- 1/4 tsp garlic powder (optional)
- 5 C. oyster crackers

Directions

- Set your oven to 250 degrees F before doing anything else.
- In a large bowl, mix together the dressing mix, dill weed, vegetable oil, lemon pepper and garlic powder.
- Add oyster crackers and toss to coat well.
- Arrange the crackers onto a baking sheet evenly.
- Cook in the oven for about 15-20 minutes.
- Remove from the oven and keep aside to cool completely before serving.

Amount per serving 20

Timing Information:

Preparation	10 m
Cooking	20 m
Total Time	45 m

Nutritional Information:

Calories	137 kcal
Fat	7 g
Carbohydrates	16.2g
Protein	1.9 g
Cholesterol	0 mg
Sodium	558 mg

* Percent Daily Values are based on a 2,000 calorie diet.

Spicy Alabama Crackers

Ingredients

- 1 2/3 C. vegetable oil
- 1 tsp garlic powder
- 1 tsp onion powder
- 1/2 tsp black pepper
- 2 (1 oz.) envelopes ranch dressing mix
- 3 tbsp crushed red pepper flakes
- 1 (16.5 oz.) package multigrain saltine crackers

Directions

- In a 2-gallon plastic zipper bag, add the vegetable oil, garlic powder, onion powder, black pepper, ranch dressing mix, and crushed red pepper flakes.
- Seal the bag and with your hands, crush the mixture to combine well.
- Now add the crackers into the bag.
- Seal the bag and shake to coat the crackers with the spice mixture evenly.
- Keep aside for about 1 hour, then shake again.
- Repeat the shaking process many times till the crackers are coated with the spice mixture generously.

- Keep aside for overnight.
- Remove the crackers from the bag and serve.

Amount per serving 30

Timing Information:

Preparation	15 m
Total Time	8 h 15 m

Nutritional Information:

Calories	181 kcal
Fat	13.9 g
Carbohydrates	12.5g
Protein	1.2 g
Cholesterol	0 mg
Sodium	320 mg

* Percent Daily Values are based on a 2,000 calorie diet.

August's Carnival Cracker Candy

Ingredients

- 1 (10 oz.) package saltine crackers
- 1 1/2 C. butter
- 1 1/2 C. packed brown sugar
- 2 (12 oz.) packages semisweet chocolate chips
- 2 C. chopped almonds

Directions

- Set your oven to 400 degrees F before doing anything else and line a 15x10-inch baking sheet with a piece of the foil.
- Arrange the crackers onto the red cookie sheet in a single layer.
- In a small pan and add the butter and brown sugar on low heat and bring to a boil.
- Boil for about 3 minutes.
- Place the sugar mixture over the crackers.
- Cook in the oven for about 5 minutes.
- Remove from the oven and immediately, spread the chocolate chips over the baked crackers evenly to melt.

- Sprinkle the almonds over the chocolate chips and with the back of a wooden spoon, press the almonds into the melted chocolate.
- Refrigerate to chill for at least 3 hours.
- Now, break into pieces and preserve in the refrigerator by placing in an airtight container.

Amount per serving 30

Timing Information:

Preparation	10 m
Cooking	10 m
Total Time	20 m

Nutritional Information:

Calories	181 kcal
Fat	13.9 g
Carbohydrates	12.5g
Protein	1.2 g
Cholesterol	0 mg
Sodium	320 mg

* Percent Daily Values are based on a 2,000 calorie diet.

Red Pepper Ranch Saltines

Ingredients

- 1 (16 oz.) package unsalted saltine crackers
- 1 C. canola oil
- 2 tsp crushed red pepper flakes
- 1 (1 oz.) package dry ranch salad dressing mix

Directions

- Unwrap the crackers and transfer into a 1 gallon size glass jar with a tight fitting lid.
- In a small bowl, add the canola oil, red pepper flakes and ranch dressing mix and stir to combine.
- Place the oil mixture over the crackers in the jar.
- Close the lid tightly and shake well.
- Keep aside for about 1 hour, shaking after every 5 minutes.

Amount per serving 16

Timing Information:

Preparation	5 m
Total Time	5 m

Nutritional Information:

Calories	253 kcal
Fat	17.4 g
Carbohydrates	21.4g
Protein	2.7 g
Cholesterol	0 mg
Sodium	340 mg

* Percent Daily Values are based on a 2,000 calorie diet.

TWO CHEESE OLIVE SPREAD

Ingredients

- 1 (8 oz.) package cream cheese, softened
- 1 (8 oz.) package finely shredded sharp Cheddar cheese
- 1/2 C. mayonnaise
- 3/4 C. chopped pimento-stuffed olives
- 1/2 C. chopped celery
- 1/3 C. chopped onion
- 1/4 C. chopped green bell pepper
- 2 tsp dried parsley

Directions

- In a bowl, add the cream cheese, Cheddar cheese and mayonnaise and with an electric mixer, beat till smooth.
- Fold in the olives, celery, onion, bell pepper and parsley.
- Refrigerate, covered for at least 1 hour.

Amount per serving 20

Timing Information:

Preparation	20 m
Total Time	1 h 20 m

Nutritional Information:

Calories	134 kcal
Fat	12.9 g
Carbohydrates	1.2g
Protein	3.9 g
Cholesterol	26 mg
Sodium	310 mg

* Percent Daily Values are based on a 2,000 calorie diet.

THE QUEEN'S COOKIES

Ingredients

- 35 soda crackers
- 1 C. butter
- 1 C. semisweet chocolate chips
- 3/4 C. finely chopped walnuts
- 1 C. packed brown sugar

Directions

- Set your oven to 375 degrees F before doing anything else and line a 15x10-inch baking sheet with a greased piece of the foil.
- Arrange the soda crackers in the prepared baking sheet.
- In a pan, melt the butter.
- Add the brown sugar and cook till the sugar dissolves, stirring continuously.
- Bring to a boil and cook for about 3 minutes, stirring continuously.
- Immediately, place the sugar mixture over the soda crackers evenly.
- Cook in the oven for about 3-5 minutes.

- Remove from the oven and immediately, spread the chocolate chips over the baked crackers evenly to melt.
- Sprinkle the walnuts over the chocolate chips and with the back of a wooden spoon, press the almonds into the melted chocolate.
- Keep aside to cool completely.
- Cut into desired sized bars and serve.

Amount per serving 18

Timing Information:

Preparation	10m
Total Time	35m

Nutritional Information:

Calories	239 kcal
Fat	17 g
Carbohydrates	22.7g
Protein	1.8 g
Cholesterol	27 mg
Sodium	140 mg

* Percent Daily Values are based on a 2,000 calorie diet.

HOMEMADE GRAHAM CRACKER CRUST 101

Ingredients

- 1 1/2 C. graham cracker crumbs
- 6 tbsp butter, softened
- 1/3 C. white sugar

Directions

- In a bowl, mix together the crumbs, butter and sugar.
- Place the crumb mixture into a 9-inch pie plate and with the back of a spoon, smooth the mixture to the side and top of the pie plate.
- Refrigerate for at least 1 hour before filling.

Amount per serving (8

Timing Information:

Preparation	5 m
Total Time	1 h 5 m

Nutritional Information:

Calories	175 kcal
Fat	10.2 g
Carbohydrates	20.4g
Protein	1.2 g
Cholesterol	23 mg
Sodium	157 mg

* Percent Daily Values are based on a 2,000 calorie diet.

SWAP CRACKERS

Ingredients

- 2 (12 oz.) packages oyster crackers
- 1 C. vegetable oil
- 1 1/2 tbsp dry Ranch-style dressing mix
- 1 tsp lemon pepper
- 1 tsp dried dill weed
- 1/2 tsp garlic salt

Directions

- In a large bowl, add the crackers and oil and toss to coat well.
- Add the dressing mix, lemon pepper, dill and salt and toss to coat well.
- Preserve these crackers in the refrigerator by placing in an airtight container.

Amount per serving 24

Timing Information:

Preparation	15 m
Total Time	15 m

Nutritional Information:

Calories	210 kcal
Fat	14.1 g
Carbohydrates	18.5g
Protein	2.3 g
Cholesterol	0 mg
Sodium	623 mg

* Percent Daily Values are based on a 2,000 calorie diet.

Sophia's Stuffing Recipe

Ingredients

- 1 (16 oz.) package milk crackers
- 1 lb. ground pork sausage
- 1 large onion, finely chopped
- 5 stalks celery, finely chopped
- 1 tsp poultry seasoning
- salt and pepper to taste
- 3 eggs, beaten
- 3 C. hot milk

Directions

- In a food processor, add the milk crackers and pulse till changes into the crumbs.
- Transfer the crumb mixture in a large bowl.
- Heat a large skillet on medium-high heat and cook the sausage till browned completely.
- Drain the grease from the skillet, reserving into a bowl.
- Add the sausage into the bowl with the crumbs and mix well.
- In a medium pan, heat 3 tbsp of the reserved grease on medium heat and sauté the onion and celery till tender.

- Transfer the onion mixture into the bowl with the crumb mixture.
- Add the poultry seasoning, salt, pepper, eggs and milk and mix well.
- Refrigerate for at least 1 hour before stuffing the turkey.

Amount per serving 10

Timing Information:

Preparation	15 m
Cooking	15 m
Total Time	30 m

Nutritional Information:

Calories	257 kcal
Fat	21.3 g
Carbohydrates	6.1g
Protein	9.9 g
Cholesterol	93 mg
Sodium	371 mg

* Percent Daily Values are based on a 2,000 calorie diet.

ARMENIAN STYLE BREAD

Ingredients

- 1 C. lukewarm water
- 1/4 C. whole wheat flour
- 1 (.25 oz.) envelope active dry yeast
- 1 tsp salt
- 3 C. all-purpose flour

Directions

- In a large bowl, add the water, whole wheat flour and yeast and mix till moistened.
- Add the salt and 1 C. of the all-purpose flour and mix.
- Slowly, add the remaining all-purpose flour and with a mixer with a dough hook attachment, mix till a dough forms.
- Place the dough onto a floured surface and knead till an elastic ball forms.
- Grease a bowl with a little bit of oil.
- Transfer the dough ball in the greased bowl and turn to coat evenly.
- Cover the bowl and keep in a warm place for about 1 hour.
- Now, with your hands, punch down the dough.

- Divide the dough into 30 walnut sized pieces and then shape each piece into a ball.
- With a damp kitchen towel, cover the balls and keep aside for about 30 minutes.
- Set your oven to 500 degrees F.
- Arrange a baking sheet over the center rack in the oven so it can preheat at the same time.
- Roll each ball into an 8-inch circle.
- Pull out the oven rack and arrange the crackers in batches onto heated baking sheet.
- Cook in the oven for about 3 minutes.
- Repeat with the remaining circles.

Amount per serving 30

Timing Information:

Preparation	15 m
Cooking	3 m
Total Time	1 h 48 m

Nutritional Information:

Calories	50 kcal
Fat	0.2 g
Carbohydrates	10.4g
Protein	1.5 g
Cholesterol	0 mg
Sodium	78 mg

* Percent Daily Values are based on a 2,000 calorie diet.

NETFLIX AND CHILL TREAT

Ingredients

- 11 C. popped popcorn
- 1 C. Spanish peanuts
- 1 1/4 C. dark brown sugar
- 10 tbsp unsalted butter, cut into pieces
- 1/4 C. dark corn syrup
- 1 tsp kosher salt

Directions

- Set your oven to 250 degrees F before doing anything else.
- In the bottom of a large, deep roasting pan, spread the popcorn and sprinkle with the peanuts.
- In a pan, mix together the brown sugar, butter, corn syrup and salt on medium-high heat and cook for about 2-3 minutes, beating continuously.
- Place the caramel sauce over the popcorn and peanuts and stir to coat completely.
- Cook in the oven for about 45 minutes, stirring occasionally.

- Remove from the oven and transfer the popcorn mixture onto a parchment paper in a single layer to cool completely.

Amount per serving 11

Timing Information:

Preparation	15 m
Cooking	50 m
Total Time	1 h 35 m

Nutritional Information:

Calories	349 kcal
Fat	21.8 g
Carbohydrates	37.4g
Protein	4.4 g
Cholesterol	28 mg
Sodium	314 mg

* Percent Daily Values are based on a 2,000 calorie diet.

HOW TO MAKE CRACKER COOKIES

Ingredients

- 1 C. butter
- 1 C. white sugar
- 1 C. packed brown sugar
- 2 eggs
- 1 tsp vanilla extract
- 1 1/2 C. all-purpose flour
- 1 tsp baking soda
- 1 tsp baking powder
- 1 pinch salt
- 2 C. quick cooking oats
- 1 1/2 C. flaked coconut
- 2 C. crisp rice cereal
- 1 1/2 C. chopped salted peanuts

Directions

- Set your oven to 350 degrees F before doing anything else and grease the baking sheets.
- In a bowl, add the butter, white sugar and brown sugar and beat till creamy.
- Add the eggs, one at a time, beating continuously.

- Add the vanilla and stir to combine.
- In another bowl, sift together the flour, baking soda, baking powder and salt.
- Add the flour mixture into the butter mixture and stir to combine.
- Gently, fold in the oatmeal, coconut, rice cereal and chopped peanuts.
- With tsp, place the mixture onto the prepared baking sheets.
- Cook in the oven for about 10-12 minutes.
- Remove from the oven and keep aside to cool completely before serving.

Amount per serving 36

Timing Information:

Preparation	30m
Cooking	12m
Total Time	42m

Nutritional Information:

Calories	186 kcal
Fat	9.6 g
Carbohydrates	22.9g
Protein	3.2 g
Cholesterol	24 mg
Sodium	165 mg

* Percent Daily Values are based on a 2,000 calorie diet.

LUMBERJACK'S SNACK

Ingredients

- 1 1/2 (8 oz.) packages thin round wheat crackers (such as Dare Breton(R)) Original Crackers)
- 1 C. butter
- 1 C. brown sugar
- 1 C. chocolate chips
- 1/2 C. chopped walnuts (optional)

Directions

- Set your oven to 350 degrees F before doing anything else and line a baking sheet with a piece of the foil.
- Arrange the crackers onto the prepared baking sheet in a single layer.
- In a pan, melt the butter and brown sugar on medium heat.
- Bring to a boil and cook for about 3 minutes.
- Place the butter mixture over the crackers evenly.
- Cook in the oven for about 15 minutes.
- Remove from oven and immediately, spread the chocolate chips on top evenly.
- Keep aside for about 2 minutes to melt.

- Spread the melted chocolate over the crackers evenly and sprinkle with the walnuts.
- Keep aside for about 1 hour to cool.
- Break into desired sized chunks and preserve these strips in the refrigerator by placing in an airtight container.

Amount per serving 20

Timing Information:

Preparation	10 m
Cooking	20 m
Total Time	1 h 30 m

Nutritional Information:

Calories	263 kcal
Fat	17.1 g
Carbohydrates	27.4g
Protein	2.4 g
Cholesterol	24 mg
Sodium	204 mg

* Percent Daily Values are based on a 2,000 calorie diet.

November's Cracker Dressing

Ingredients

- cooking spray
- 1/2 C. butter
- 1 large onion, diced
- 3 stalks celery, diced
- 1 tsp salt, or to taste
- 1/2 tsp freshly ground black pepper
- 1/2 tsp dried sage
- 1/2 tsp dried thyme
- 1/2 tsp dried rosemary
- 1 pinch cayenne pepper
- 2 3/4 C. chicken broth
- 1 lb. saltine crackers, crushed
- 1/2 C. milk
- 1 egg

Directions

- Set your oven to 375 degrees F before doing anything else and lightly, grease a baking dish with the cooking spray.

- In a large skillet, melt the butter on medium heat and sauté the onion, celery and 1 tsp of the salt for about 5 minutes.
- Stir in the black pepper, sage, thyme, rosemary and cayenne pepper and sauté for about 1 minute.
- Remove the skillet from the heat and stir in the chicken broth.
- In a large bowl, mix together the crushed crackers and onion mixture.
- Add the egg and cream and mix till well combined.
- Stir in the salt and black pepper.
- In a large baking dish, place the cracker mixture evenly and with the back of a spoon, smooth the top surface.
- Cook in the oven for about 40-45 minutes.

Amount per serving 16

Timing Information:

Preparation	20 m
Cooking	50 m
Total Time	1 h 10 m

Nutritional Information:

Calories	189 kcal
Fat	9.6 g
Carbohydrates	21.9g
Protein	3.7 g
Cholesterol	28 mg
Sodium	670 mg

* Percent Daily Values are based on a 2,000 calorie diet.

MONROE STREET CRACKERS

Ingredients

- 1/2 tsp vegetable oil
- 2 tbsp unsalted butter at room temperature
- 3/4 C. lightly packed shredded sharp Cheddar cheese
- 1/3 C. lightly packed freshly shredded Parmesan cheese
- 1/2 tsp paprika
- 1 pinch cayenne pepper
- 1/4 tsp salt
- 1/2 C. all-purpose flour
- 1 tbsp cold water

Directions

- In a bowl, add the butter, Cheddar cheese, Parmesan cheese, paprika, cayenne pepper, and salt and with the back of a spatula, mix till well combined.
- Add the flour and with a fork, mix till crumbly.
- Slowly, drizzle with the cold water, 1-2 drops at a time and with a spatula, mix till a dough forms.
- Place the dough onto a smooth surface and press into a thick, flattened disk.

- With a plastic wrap, cover the dough disk and refrigerate for about 30 minutes.
- Set your oven to 375 degrees F and line a baking sheet with a piece of the foil and then lightly grease with the vegetable oil.
- Place the dough onto a floured smooth surface and roll into about 1/8-inch thickness.
- With a pizza cutter, cut the dough into 1-inch wide strips and then cut into about 1 1/2-inch long rectangles crosswise.
- With the back of a bamboo skewer, punch 5 small holes into each cracker.
- Place the crackers onto the prepared baking sheet.
- Cook in the oven for about 15 minutes.
- Remove from the oven and keep aside for about 3 minutes to cool.
- Remove from the foil and keep aside to cool completely before serving.

Amount per serving 36

Timing Information:

Preparation	20 m
Cooking	15 m
Total Time	1 h 20 m

Nutritional Information:

Calories	25 kcal
Fat	1.7 g
Carbohydrates	1.4g
Protein	1.1 g
Cholesterol	5 mg
Sodium	43 mg

* Percent Daily Values are based on a 2,000 calorie diet.

Buttery Goobers

Ingredients

- 12 whole graham crackers
- 1 C. margarine
- 1 C. brown sugar
- 1 C. chopped pecans

Directions

- Set your oven to 350 degrees F before doing anything else.
- Break each graham cracker into 4 equal sized pieces, creating 48 total.
- Arrange the graham cracker pieces onto a baking sheet about closely together.
- In a heavy pan, melt the margarine on medium heat.
- Add the brown sugar and cook till boiling and frothy, stirring continuously.
- Boil for about 2 minutes, stirring continuously.
- Remove from the heat and fold in the pecans.
- Place the caramel mixture over the crackers evenly.
- Cook in the oven for about 8-10 minutes.
- Remove from the oven and immediately, transfer onto a piece of foil to cool.

Amount per serving 24

Timing Information:

Preparation	20 m
Cooking	10 m
Total Time	30 m

Nutritional Information:

Calories	163 kcal
Fat	11.5 g
Carbohydrates	15.1g
Protein	1 g
Cholesterol	0 mg
Sodium	133 mg

* Percent Daily Values are based on a 2,000 calorie diet.

2 INGREDIENT CRACKERS

Ingredients

- 24 saltine crackers
- 6 slices American cheese

Directions

- Set your oven to 450 degrees F before doing anything else.
- Arrange the crackers onto a baking sheet in a single layer, keeping some space between each other.
- Fold each piece of the American cheese in half.
- Fold each half of the American cheese in half, creating 24 squares.
- Arrange 1 cheese square over each cracker.
- Cook in the oven for about 3-5 minutes.
- Remove from the oven and keep aside to cool completely before serving.

Amount per serving 6

Timing Information:

Preparation	10 m
Cooking	3 m
Total Time	13 m

Nutritional Information:

Calories	158 kcal
Fat	10.2 g
Carbohydrates	9g
Protein	7.4 g
Cholesterol	27 mg
Sodium	551 mg

* Percent Daily Values are based on a 2,000 calorie diet.

MATZO MEAL CRACKERS

Ingredients

- 1 (8 oz.) container cottage cheese
- 1/4 C. matzo meal
- 1/4 C. white sugar
- 1/2 tsp salt
- 40 whole saltine crackers
- 2 eggs
- 1/4 C. vegetable oil

Directions

- In a bowl, mix together the cottage cheese, matzo meal, sugar and salt.
- Place about 1 tbsp of the cheese mixture over a cracker of half the crackers and top with the remaining crackers to make a sandwich.
- In a shallow bowl, beat the eggs.
- Coat the cracker sandwich in beaten egg evenly.
- In a large skillet, heat the vegetable oil on medium heat and fry the cracker sandwiches for about 1-2 minutes per side.
- Serve these sandwiches hot.

Amount per serving 10

Timing Information:

Preparation	15 m
Cooking	10 m
Total Time	25 m

Nutritional Information:

Calories	124 kcal
Fat	3.9 g
Carbohydrates	16.9g
Protein	5.5 g
Cholesterol	41 mg
Sodium	350 mg

* Percent Daily Values are based on a 2,000 calorie diet.

CONDENSED CHOCOLATE CHIP CRACKERS

Ingredients

- 1 (12 oz.) bag milk chocolate chips
- 2 (14 oz.) cans sweetened condensed milk
- 1 (14.4 oz.) package graham cracker, crushed into fine crumbs

Directions

- In a pan, add the chocolate chips and condensed milk on low heat and cook till the chocolate is melted, stirring continuously.
- Stir in the crushed graham crackers.
- Place the mixture into a well-greased 13x9-inch glass baking dish and with the back of a spoon, smooth the surface.
- Refrigerate to cool about 2 hours before serving.

Amount per serving 30

Timing Information:

Preparation	5 m
Cooking	15 m
Total Time	2 h 20 m

Nutritional Information:

Calories	202 kcal
Fat	7.4 g
Carbohydrates	31.5g
Protein	3.8 g
Cholesterol	13 mg
Sodium	134 mg

* Percent Daily Values are based on a 2,000 calorie diet.

Australian Style Strawberry Cracker Bites

Ingredients

- 30 sliced fresh strawberries
- 1 (7 oz.) can whipped cream
- 1 (13 oz.) jar chocolate-hazelnut spread (such as Nutella(R))
- 30 fresh blueberries
- 1 (14.4 oz.) package mini graham crackers

Directions

- Cut the bottom of each strawberry and hollow out the top.
- In a bowl, mix together the whipped cream and chocolate-hazelnut spread.
- Fill the hollow part of each strawberry with the whipped cream mixture and top with 1 blueberry.
- Top each filled strawberry with a mini graham cracker.

Amount per serving 30

Timing Information:

Preparation	20 m
Total Time	20 m

Nutritional Information:

Calories	144 kcal
Fat	6.4 g
Carbohydrates	20.3g
Protein	2.1 g
Cholesterol	5 mg
Sodium	103 mg

* Percent Daily Values are based on a 2,000 calorie diet.

3 INGREDIENT RANCH CRACKERS

Ingredients

- 1 (1 oz.) package ranch dressing mix
- 1 1/2 C. vegetable oil
- 1 (16 oz.) package saltine crackers

Directions

- In a 2-gallon resealable bag, place the ranch dressing mix and vegetable oil.
- Seal the bag and shake till well combined.
- Add the crackers and shake till the crackers are coated completely.
- Keep aside for about 3 hours, shaking after every 1/2 hour.

Amount per serving 15

Timing Information:

Preparation	5 m
Cooking	3 h 5 m
Total Time	5 m

Nutritional Information:

Calories	325 kcal
Fat	25.2 g
Carbohydrates	22.1g
Protein	2.8 g
Cholesterol	0 mg
Sodium	451 mg

* Percent Daily Values are based on a 2,000 calorie diet.

MEMPHIS INSPIRED STRAWBERRY CRACKER PIE

Ingredients

- 3 egg whites
- 1 C. white sugar
- 1/2 tsp baking powder
- 1/4 tsp salt
- 1 tsp vanilla extract
- 14 buttery round crackers, crushed
- 2/3 C. chopped pecans
- 1 (8 oz.) container frozen whipped topping, thawed
- 2 C. fresh strawberries, sliced

Directions

- Set your oven to 350 degrees F before doing anything else and grease a 9-inch pie dish.
- In a large glass bowl, add the egg whites and beat till foamy.
- Slowly, add the sugar, baking powder, salt and vanilla, beating continuously till the stiff peaks form.
- Gently fold in the crackers and pecans.

- Place the mixture into the prepared pie dish.
- Cook in the oven for about 30 minutes.
- Remove from the oven and keep aside to cool.
- Refrigerate, covered for overnight.
- Just before serving, spread the whipped topping over the pie.
- Serve with a topping of the strawberry slices.

Amount per serving 6

Timing Information:

Preparation	15 m
Cooking	30 m
Total Time	45 m

Nutritional Information:

Calories	387 kcal
Fat	17.4 g
Carbohydrates	52.7g
Protein	3.8 g
Cholesterol	0 mg
Sodium	230 mg

* Percent Daily Values are based on a 2,000 calorie diet.

VANILLA CRACKER SPREAD

Ingredients

- 2 graham crackers, crumbled
- 1/4 C. brown sugar
- 1/8 tsp ground cinnamon
- 2 tbsp melted butter
- 1 tsp vanilla
- 2 tbsp white sugar
- 1 dash salt

Directions

- Set your oven to 375 degrees F before doing anything else and grease a small baking dish.
- In a small bowl, mix together the crumbled graham crackers, brown sugar and cinnamon.
- Add the melted butter and vanilla and stir to combine.
- Place the mixture into the prepared dish evenly and sprinkle with the white sugar and salt.
- Cook in the oven for about 15 minutes.

Amount per serving 2

Timing Information:

Preparation	5 m
Cooking	15 m
Total Time	20 m

Nutritional Information:

Calories	321 kcal
Fat	12.9 g
Carbohydrates	50.6g
Protein	1.1 g
Cholesterol	31 mg
Sodium	368 mg

* Percent Daily Values are based on a 2,000 calorie diet.

CHIPOTLE CRACKERS

Ingredients

- 3 C. all-purpose flour
- 2/3 C. flax seeds
- 1/3 C. chia seeds
- 1 1/2 tsp baking powder
- 1/2 tsp salt
- 1/2 tsp garlic powder
- 1/2 tsp onion powder
- 1/4 tsp ground dried chipotle pepper
- 1/2 C. unsalted butter
- 1 C. water
- 2 tbsp olive oil

Directions

- Set your oven to 400 degrees F before doing anything else and grease 2 baking sheets.
- In a large bowl, mix together the flour, flax seeds, chia seeds, baking powder, salt, garlic powder, onion powder and dried chipotle pepper powder.
- With a pastry cutter, cut butter into flour mixture till a coarse crumbs like mixture forms.

- Add the water and olive oil and with a fork, mix till a sticky dough forms.
- Divide the dough into 2 equal sized portions.
- Place the dough portions onto a floured smooth surface and roll out as thin as possible.
- Cut each dough portion into squares.
- Arrange the squares onto prepared baking sheet.
- Cook in the oven for about 8 minutes.
- Remove from the oven and keep aside to cool completely before serving.

Amount per serving 8

Timing Information:

Preparation	15 m
Cooking	10 m
Total Time	40 m

Nutritional Information:

Calories	397 kcal
Fat	22.3 g
Carbohydrates	42.2g
Protein	8.1 g
Cholesterol	31 mg
Sodium	245 mg

* Percent Daily Values are based on a 2,000 calorie diet.

SOPHISTICATED PECAN GRAHAM CRACKERS

Ingredients

- 1/2 C. butter
- 1/2 C. margarine
- 1 C. brown sugar
- 24 graham crackers, broken into rectangles
- 1 C. chopped pecans

Directions

- Set your oven to 350 degrees F before doing anything else and line a jelly roll pan with a piece of the foil.
- In a pan, melt the butter and margarine.
- Add the brown sugar into the butter mixture and stir till sugar is dissolved.
- Bring to a boil, stirring continuously.
- Reduce the heat to medium and cook at a boil for about 2 minutes.
- I the bottom of the prepared pan, place the graham crackers in a single layer.
- Place the butter mixture over the crackers evenly and sprinkle with the pecans.

- Cook in the oven for about 12 minutes.
- Remove from the oven and keep aside to cool completely before breaking into pieces.

Amount per serving 48

Timing Information:

Preparation	10 m
Cooking	20 m
Total Time	30 m

Nutritional Information:

Calories	76 kcal
Fat	5.8 g
Carbohydrates	6g
Protein	0.5 g
Cholesterol	5 mg
Sodium	58 mg

* Percent Daily Values are based on a 2,000 calorie diet.

BROWN RICE AND QUINOA CRACKERS

Ingredients

- 1 C. cooked brown rice
- 1 C. cooked quinoa
- 2 tsp tamari (gluten-free soy sauce) (optional)
- 1 tbsp water, or as needed (optional)
- 1/4 C. chia seeds
- 1/4 C. sesame seeds
- 1/4 C. flax seeds
- salt to taste

Directions

- Set your oven to 350 degrees F before doing anything else and line a baking sheet with the parchment paper.
- Cut a small square from another parchment paper and grease 1 side of it.
- In a food processor, add the brown rice, quinoa and tamari and pulse till a dough begins to form. (You can add water if mixture is too dry.)
- Add chia seeds, sesame seeds, flax seeds, and salt and pulse till a sticky dough forms.

- Divide the dough into small pieces and then roll each piece into 1/2-inch ball.
- Arrange the balls onto the prepared baking sheet about 2 1/2-inch apart.
- Place the greased parchment square, oil-side down over a dough ball.
- With the top of a small jar, flatten the ball into a very thin 2-inch-wide disk.
- Repeat with the remaining dough balls.
- Cook in the oven for about 10-12 minutes.
- Remove from the oven and transfer the crackers onto a wire rack.
- Arrange the rack onto the baking sheet and cook in the oven for about 2-3 minutes more.

Amount per serving 8

Timing Information:

Preparation	15 m
Cooking	15 m
Total Time	30 m

Nutritional Information:

Calories	126 kcal
Fat	6.1 g
Carbohydrates	14.8g
Protein	4 g
Cholesterol	0 mg
Sodium	108 mg

* Percent Daily Values are based on a 2,000 calorie diet.

THE PEOPLE'S REPUBLIC OF CRACKERS

Ingredients

- 1/2 C. water
- 1/4 C. teff flour
- 3 tbsp tapioca flour
- 1/4 C. sunflower seed kernels
- 1/4 C. pepitas (roasted green pumpkin seeds)
- 1 tbsp sesame seeds
- 1 tbsp flax seeds
- 1 tbsp teff
- 1 tsp black sesame seeds
- 1/4 tsp salt
- salt to taste

Directions

- Set your oven to 375 degrees F before doing anything else and grease a 12x9-inch baking sheet.
- In a bowl, add the water, teff flour and tapioca flour and mix till smooth.
- Add the sunflower seeds, pepitas, sesame seeds, flax seeds, teff, black sesame seeds, and 1/4 tsp of the salt and stir till a soupy mixture forms.

- Place the mixture onto the prepared baking sheet evenly.
- Cook in the oven for about 40 minutes.
- Remove from the oven and keep aside to cool slightly.
- Sprinkle salt over the warm crackers and serve.

Amount per serving 4

Timing Information:

Preparation	10 m
Cooking	40 m
Total Time	50 m

Nutritional Information:

Calories	161 kcal
Fat	8.5 g
Carbohydrates	18.3g
Protein	4.9 g
Cholesterol	0 mg
Sodium	247 mg

* Percent Daily Values are based on a 2,000 calorie diet.

ITALIAN FESTIVAL PUDDING

Ingredients

- 2 eggs, separated
- 1/2 C. white sugar
- 4 C. 2% milk
- 1 C. flaked coconut
- 2 C. crushed saltine crackers
- 1 tsp vanilla extract

Directions

- In a bowl, add the egg yolks and sugar and with an electric mixer, beat till fluffy and pale yellow.
- In a large pan, heat the milk on medium heat.
- Add the egg yolk mixture and beat till smooth.
- Boil for about 1 minute, stirring continuously.
- Stir in the coconut and cracker crumbs and bring to a boil.
- Reduce the heat to low and simmer for about 5 minutes.
- In a glass bowl, add the egg whites and with an electric mixer, beat till stiff peaks form.
- Gently fold in the coconut mixture.
- Add the vanilla extract and stir to combine.
- This pudding can be served warm or cold as well.

Amount per serving 6

Timing Information:

Preparation	15 m
Cooking	10 m
Total Time	25 m

Nutritional Information:

Calories	328 kcal
Fat	11 g
Carbohydrates	47.4g
Protein	10 g
Cholesterol	75 mg
Sodium	375 mg

* Percent Daily Values are based on a 2,000 calorie diet.

ICE CREAM GRAHAM CRACKER FLAVORED

Ingredients

- 2 C. fat free half-and-half
- 1/2 C. sugar
- 1/2 vanilla bean
- 3 fat-free graham crackers, crushed

Directions

- In a large bowl, add the half-and-half and sugar and mix till well combined.
- Split the vanilla bean lengthwise and scrape the seeds.
- Add the vanilla bean seeds into the bowl with the sugar mixture and beat till well combined.
- Transfer the mixture into an ice cream maker and process according to manufacturer's directions.
- After the mixture becomes semi-frozen, sprinkle the crushed graham crackers over the mixture.
- Process till desired consistency.

Amount per serving 8

Timing Information:

Preparation	30 m
Total Time	30 m

Nutritional Information:

Calories	94 kcal
Fat	1 g
Carbohydrates	19.9g
Protein	1.7 g
Cholesterol	3 mg
Sodium	92 mg

* Percent Daily Values are based on a 2,000 calorie diet.

LISSETTE'S CRACKERS

Ingredients

- 2 C. ground flaxseed
- 1 C. cashews
- 1 red bell pepper, halved and deseeded
- 1 carrot
- 1 clove garlic
- 1 lemon, juiced
- 1/2 tsp sea salt
- 1/2 tsp agave nectar

Directions

- In a food processor, add the flaxseed, cashews, red bell pepper, carrot, garlic, lemon juice, sea salt and agave nectar and pulse till smooth.
- Spread the pureed mixture onto the nonstick food dehydrator sheets.
- Place the dehydrator sheets into the food dehydrator according to manufacturer's directions.
- Dehydrate for about 18 hours, flipping once after 6 hours.
- Break the sheets into desired sized pieces and serve.

Amount per serving 12

Timing Information:

Preparation	15 m
Total Time	18 h 15 m

Nutritional Information:

Calories	210 kcal
Fat	16.2 g
Carbohydrates	12.6g
Protein	6.6 g
Cholesterol	0 mg
Sodium	158 mg

* Percent Daily Values are based on a 2,000 calorie diet.

CAKE A LA CRACKERS

Ingredients

- 6 egg whites
- 1 tsp cream of tartar
- 1 tsp vanilla extract
- 2 C. white sugar
- 36 saltine crackers, finely crushed
- 2 C. chopped pecans
- 1 (20 oz.) can crushed pineapple
- 1 (8 oz.) tub frozen whipped topping, thawed

Directions

- Set your oven to 325 degrees F before doing anything else and grease a 13x9-inch baking dish.
- In a large glass bowl, add the egg whites, cream of tartar and vanilla and beat till soft peaks form.
- Slowly, add the sugar, beating till stiff peaks form.
- Fold in the cracker crumbs and pecans.
- Transfer the cracker mixture in the prepared baking dish evenly.
- Cook in the oven for about 30 minutes.

- Remove from the oven and keep aside to cool completely before frosting.
- For frosting in a bowl, mix together the crushed pineapple and whipped topping.
- Spread the frosting over the cooled cake evenly and refrigerate till serving.

Amount per serving 12

Timing Information:

Preparation	10 m
Cooking	30 m
Total Time	40 m

Nutritional Information:

Calories	402 kcal
Fat	20.1 g
Carbohydrates	54.5g
Protein	4.9 g
Cholesterol	0 mg
Sodium	130 mg

* Percent Daily Values are based on a 2,000 calorie diet.

LITTLE PIZZA CRACKERS

Ingredients

- 24 whole wheat crackers
- 1/4 C. pizza sauce
- 24 slices beef pepperoni
- 1 1/2 C. finely shredded mozzarella cheese

Directions

- Spread about 1/2 tsp of the pizza sauce over each cracker and top with a pepperoni slice.
- Sprinkle each cracker with the shredded mozzarella cheese evenly.
- In a microwave safe plate, arrange the crackers and microwave on High for about 1-2 minutes.

Amount per serving 3

Timing Information:

Preparation	5 m
Cooking	2 m
Total Time	7 m

Nutritional Information:

Calories	308 kcal
Fat	19.3 g
Carbohydrates	13.9g
Protein	19 g
Cholesterol	53 mg
Sodium	850 mg

* Percent Daily Values are based on a 2,000 calorie diet.

QUEENS BOROUGH CRACKERS

Ingredients

- 1 C. rye flour
- 1 C. all-purpose flour
- 1 tbsp caraway seed
- 1 1/2 tsp salt
- 1 tsp onion powder
- 1 tsp garlic powder
- 1/3 C. canola oil
- 1 tsp honey
- 1/4 C. water

Directions

- In a bowl, mix together the flours, caraway seed, salt, onion powder and garlic powder.
- Add the canola oil and honey and stir to combine.
- Slowly add the water, stirring with a fork till a ball like dough forms.
- Cover the dough and keep aside for about 10 minutes.
- Set your oven to 375 degrees F.
- Divide the dough into 4 equal sized portions.

- Place each dough piece onto parchment paper and roll into 1/8-inch thickness.
- Cut each dough piece into desired shape.
- Arrange the crackers onto a baking sheet and with a fork, prick each cracker a few times.
- Cook in the oven for about 10-12 minutes.
- Remove from the oven and keep aside to cool completely before serving.

Amount per serving 12

Timing Information:

Preparation	10 m
Cooking	10 m
Total Time	30 m

Nutritional Information:

Calories	129 kcal
Fat	6.5 g
Carbohydrates	15.9g
Protein	2 g
Cholesterol	0 mg
Sodium	291 mg

* Percent Daily Values are based on a 2,000 calorie diet.

LITTLE TIKE LUNCH BOX SANDWICHES

Ingredients

- 3/4 C. peanut butter
- 2 lb. chocolate-flavored almond bark
- 80 buttery round crackers
- 2 1/4 oz. colored candy sprinkles

Directions

- Spread about 1 tsp of the peanut butter over each of half of the crackers and top with the remaining crackers to make sandwiches.
- In the top of a double boiler, melt the chocolate-flavored almond bark over hot water.
- Reduce the heat and keep the chocolate in top of double boiler over simmering water.
- Coat each cracker sandwich in the melted chocolate and drain back the extra chocolate into pan.
- Place coated cracker sandwiches over the wax paper to cool completely.
- Sprinkle the cracker sandwiches with the multi-colored sprinkles and refrigerate for about 15 minutes to set completely.

- You can preserve these cracker sandwiches in the refrigerator by placing between layers of wax paper in an airtight container.

Amount per serving 20

Timing Information:

Preparation	15m
Cooking	20m
Total Time	35m

Nutritional Information:

Calories	389 kcal
Fat	24 g
Carbohydrates	39.3g
Protein	6 g
Cholesterol	10 mg
Sodium	214 mg

* Percent Daily Values are based on a 2,000 calorie diet.

THANKS FOR READING! JOIN THE CLUB AND KEEP ON COOKING WITH 6 MORE COOKBOOKS....

http://bit.ly/1TdrStv

 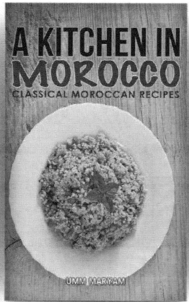 

To grab the box sets simply follow the link mentioned above, or tap one of book covers.

This will take you to a page where you can simply enter your email address and a PDF version of the box sets will be emailed to you.

Hope you are ready for some serious cooking!

http://bit.ly/1TdrStv

COME ON...
LET'S BE FRIENDS :)

We adore our readers and love connecting with them socially.

Like BookSumo on Facebook and let's get social!

Facebook

And also check out the BookSumo Cooking Blog.

Food Lover Blog

Made in the USA
Middletown, DE
22 December 2017